The Sunday Supp€
Exeter
07542 081525

Classic Lines
Devotional Insights for Women

JENNY GILPIN

All correspondence to:
Jenny Gilpin
Hope City Church,The Megacentre
Bernard Road, Sheffield, S2 5BQ
jenny.gilpin@hopecity.co.uk
www.hopecitychurch.tv

Published by Integrity Media Europe
Unit 1 Hargreaves Business Park
Hargreaves Road, Eastbourne, BN23 6QW

ISBN 978-1-907080-03-6

Classic Lines

Devotional Insights for Women

JENNY GILPIN

Jenny Gilpin began her life awaiting adoption in a hospital in Queensland, Australia. At sixteen years of age her adopted dad passed away, and she wondered about her real father. After leaving the beautiful shores of Australia at the age of twenty five to pursue a dream to touch Great Britain with the Gospel, she heard news that, for the first time, she was able to meet her real mother. Upon that dramatic encounter, she learned that she was the outcome of a gang rape. With a shattered dream of finding fatherhood she leaned all of her heart onto her ever increasing revelation of the Father heart of God.

'Classic Lines' is infused with the certainty and knowledge that all of us originated from the heart of our Heavenly Father. None of us can ever escape His loving gaze and willing spirit to lead us and love on us all the days of our lives.

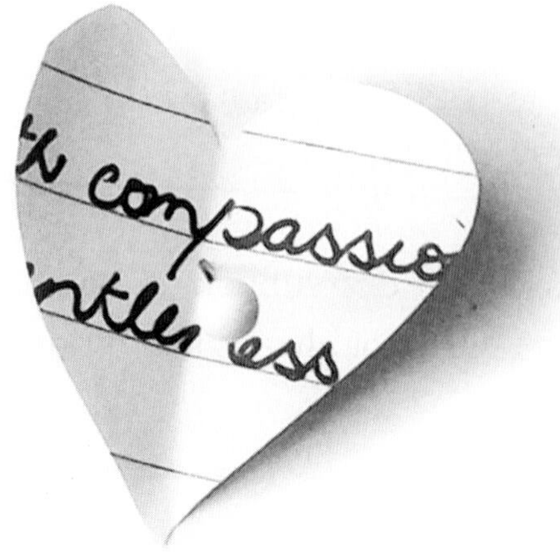
compassio

Dedication

I would like to dedicate this book to Enid Stewart.
Her hunger for God rubbed off on me at an early age.
Thank you mum for always teaching me to be gracious.

those who follow us can only have what we are

Children become who their parents are - not what they do. So much of what comes out of our lives is caught not taught. Our prayer must be that this contagious condition, this hope in Christ, that we are incubating breeds faith, hope and goodness to all who follow behind us. We are constantly responsible for increasing our own capacity to carry weight. The bigger we are, the more we hold. The more we hold, the more we can give. Because we give what we are, not what we know, more can be caught by the world that surrounds us.

2 Corinthians 2:15
"We are to God the aroma of Christ."

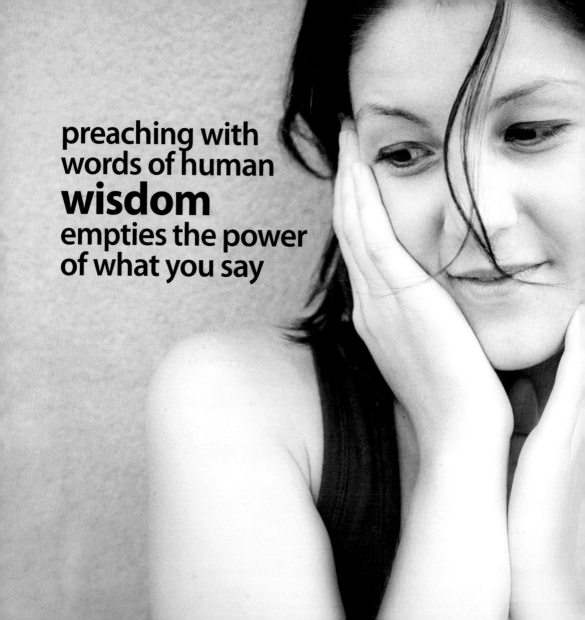

Our prayer must be that our words are full of Godly wisdom. Preaching and speaking stuff which comes out of the cleverness of our own thinking has the capacity to empty the cross of its power through our lives. Only wisdom from heaven connects with the supernatural to bring about powerful change. God's wisdom heals a wound. Worldly wisdom merely patches over a scar.

1 Corinthians 1: 17
"But to preach the gospel - not with words of human wisdom, lest the cross of Christ be emptied of its power."

It's always what sneaks up behind us that scares us. Unless we want to live life constantly looking in our rear view mirror, we need to realise that God has a shield around us. He shields our front, our sides and our back. Our past that follows us has no power over us, nor does any sneaky plan of the enemy. When you live with God as your 360 degree shield, life loses its sense of threat.

Psalm 3: 3
"But you are a shield around me."

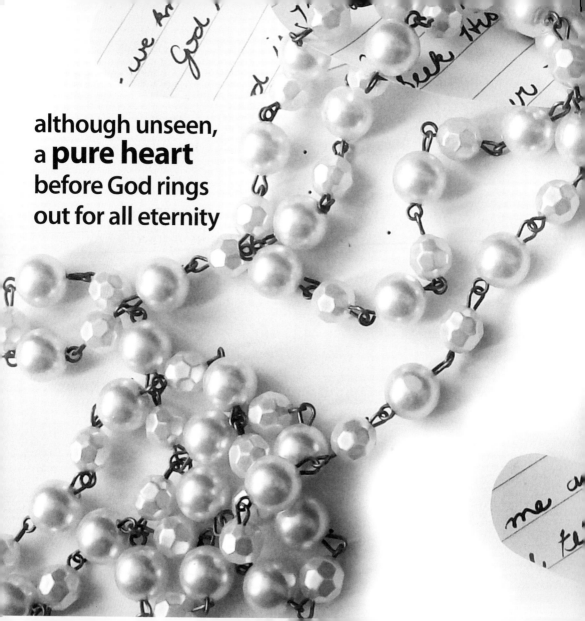

although unseen,
a **pure heart**
before God rings
out for all eternity

Although it is often a battle, fight to keep a pure heart. Fight to maintain a purity of motivation and thought that honours God. There are some things which no man can see, but which God registers in Heaven. "Above all else, guard your heart". The issues of life spring out of it and also the eternal smile of Heaven.

2 Corinthians 4:18
"...but what is unseen is eternal."

the future
is **always**
brighter

An awesome promise is that our future is going to be illuminated by an even brighter light. As we continue to walk our journey with our Father, our lives and paths become clearer and brighter. We learn not to worry about our ways, we learn just to walk in them. We don't become exempt from adversity, but God causes even our darkness to become light.

Proverbs 4:18
"The path of the righteous is like the first gleam of dawn, shining ever brighter til the full light of day."

the key to **freshness** in life is just to wake up to His new mercies every day

The key to freshness in our walk with God is not to dwell on either yesterday's successes or yesterday's failures. God has a truck-load of new mercies awaiting our lives every day when we wake up. We must not be flushed by our successes or duped by our failures. Yesterday belongs with yesterday and today is a new day of amazing mercy, grace and blessing.

Lamentations 3:22-23
"...His compassions never fail. They are new every morning."

the key to our lives is **hidden** in the secret place with God

It's not like God plays hide and seek with us, or that He hides His will and ways from us. It is just that He wants to draw us into that place where we spend time with Him - time in His secret place. It is in that secret place that God unravels our heads, deals with its complexities and unfolds the future. In that place we fall in love with God's purposes for our lives and not our own.

Proverbs 19:21
"Many are the plans in a man's heart,
but it is the Lord's purpose that prevails."

knowing you are seen by God is the basis of everything

It all starts by knowing that God actually sees the raw, vivid detail of our lives. He saw us even before we could see Him. God doesn't stop seeing our lives when He first meets us, but He continues to see all we do in detail. God is concerned about every intricate thread of your existence. He knows about you, cares about you and is a prayer away from helping you.

John 1:48
"I saw you while you were still under the fig tree, before Philip called you."

listen
to the
red light
of the Holy Spirit

Yesterday's green light may have changed colour. It may have turned amber or even red. Sensible, prudent people sensitise themselves to God changing a season in their lives. They take refuge under the shadow of His wings and await instructions. Await the green light of the Holy Spirit and never walk over a sensitised conscience.

Proverbs 27:12
"The prudent see danger and take refuge,
but the simple keep going and suffer for it."

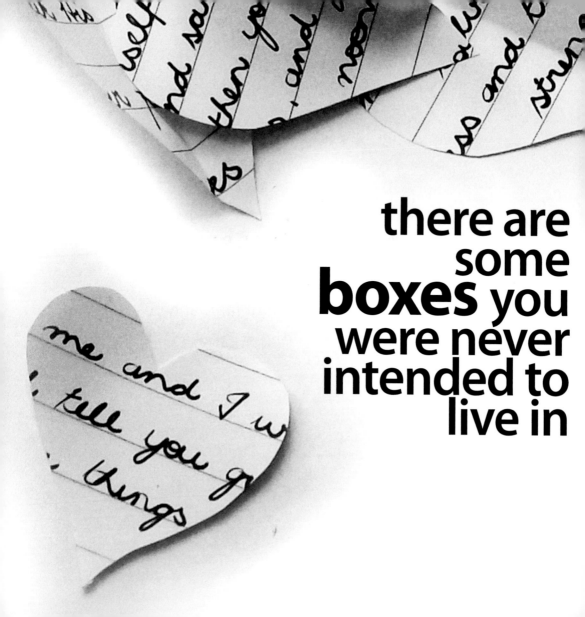

there are
some
boxes you
were never
intended to
live in

When God offers us freedom, He extends His hand for us to step out of a contained life. God never intended us to live imprisoned by boxes - boxes of fear, rejection, insecurity and pleasing public opinion. We stay too long in boxes which can easily become coffins - easy and comfortable but a place of decay! Step out of containment into a place of faith and possibility and on to a journey of adventure and excitement that is your God-given destiny.

John 8:32
"Then you will know the truth and the truth will set you free."

persecution
is norma

Remember when you are not liked or misjudged in your service for Christ that this is just normal Christian living. This is just your due service! When we are persecuted, misjudged, misunderstood and disliked we are merely going the way of Christ. We are being willing to share in the same suffering that Jesus Himself endured. The joy is knowing that God loves those who are willing to live the way Jesus did.

John 15:18-20
"If the world hates you, keep it in mind that it hated me first....
If they persecuted me, they will also persecute you."

we were never
designed for
self-sufficiency

So many of us love to lean on God but become incredibly self-sufficient when asked to interact with others. We were designed by God with a need to lean on, and to be leant upon by others. So often we abort that choice in our quest to not be too vulnerable. Vulnerability is a doorway to truly living the Christian life as God intended it to be lived. We are designed for community, family and mutual respect. It is time to lay our hurts, pride and insecurities down and choose to lean upon someone else.

Ephesians 5:21
"Submit to one another out of reverence for Christ."

the **preparation** is up to us, the move of God is up to the Maker

In our quest for God to do a new thing we sometimes try to force the hand of God. He promises that He will give us incredible fruit, even in the midst of what seems an absolute desert. He promises He will make a way and give us directions and a path onward. Our job is just to keep our hearts right and wait for His time. Get the preparation right and the move of God will follow.

Isaiah 43:19b
"I am making a way in the desert and streams in the wasteland."

God needs the water
of your present to
create the **wine** of
your future

When life feels like it is running at a very low ebb, we must remember the incredible value of that which we have in our hands right now. It is so important to treat with thankfulness the water God has given you now. This same water is the very tool God will use to turn your future into wine. Keep faithfully pouring what God has given you now into those very normal looking stone jars. They are the stone jars of faithfully serving where you are right now. It's the water in those jars that God will miraculously turn into the wine of your future.

John 2:9
"...and the master of the banquet tasted the water that had been turned into wine."

adversity
doesn't
spell
defeat

Adversity is just an elevator stop on the way up to the top. Adversity is just a base camp on the way up a mountain. Adversity is the bad exam results on the way to a masters degree. Adversity is the financial crisis on the way to resourcing God's kingdom. Adversity is the lie of the present that tries to obscure the better future. Your victory was assured before any adversity began.

Isaiah 46:11
"What I have said, that I will bring about;
what I have planned, that I will do."

treat your hard
place like a
hotel

The hard place was never intended to be a home, but a hotel. A place where we go for a visit, learn our lessons and move on. We should never treat our hard times as a place of permanent residence. They are instead launch pads where we actually learn to prosper. The children of Israel prospered during their stay in Egypt. God can cause us to prosper in our perceived prison.

Acts 13:17
"He made the people prosper during their stay in Egypt."

create a platform where people can
hear the **true whisper** of heaven

We so need to know what heaven is truly whispering about us. We need to know His voice is not one of condemnation. Instead His whisper over our lives is a whisper of incredible affection and amazing love. He whispers over our lives whispers of total acceptance, and He reminds us that a great crowd of witnesses are standing by cheering us on.

Hebrews 12:1
"Since we are surrounded by such a great crowd of witnesses, let us throw off everything that hinders..."

upgrade
to the size of
your future

It's time to pitch our lives according to the promise of the future - not the deceit of the present or the lie of the past. Retreating into your spirit is always the most easy and comfortable option, but we must not downsize in the face of difficulty. See the fact that God has already given the deliverance and victory into your hands. Respond with the eye of faith. Your future depends on what you see today.

Joshua 6:2
"See, I have delivered Jericho into your hands."

favour and **influence** are held in his hands

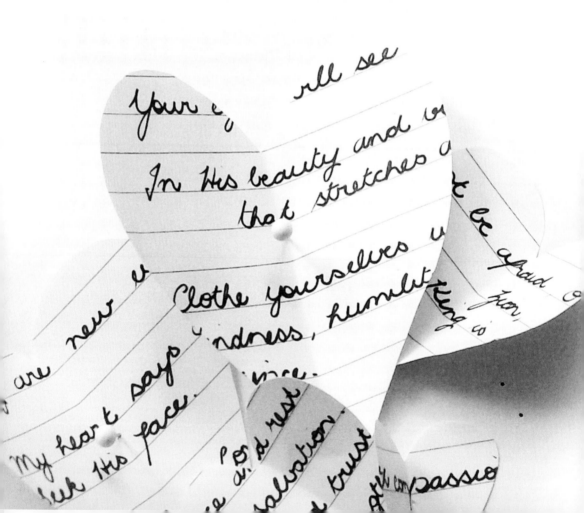

When God's favour is on something, He maintains the height, momentum and colour of His cause. He promises that He will maintain and look after those areas in our lives that His favour lies upon. We are often tempted to manufacture the duration, consistency and quality of the favour that God has towards us. We want that which we fought for and the high ground we've gained to last and endure on our terms. Hands off!

Psalm 30:7
"O Lord, when you favoured me,
You made my mountain stand firm."

the **voice**
of God
turns a
barren
place into
a place of
beauty

Hearing God's voice over a place of barrenness in your life is like cool water on a hot summer's day. God's tender voice makes something barren incredibly beautiful, caresses it back to life and breathes on it hope for the future. Only God the Holy Spirit has the supernatural ability to make that which was dead - alive again. When Jesus came back to life, not many recognised Him. Allow room for the grand re-inventions of the Spirit. Behold, He makes all things new!

Psalm 29:8
"The voice of the Lord shakes the desert."

kindness **cradles** humanity

Compassion and kindness are garments we choose to put on. We wear them as the first outfit people see. Compassion and kindness are not wishy-washy virtues. Kindness is an offensive weapon. It was Jesus' kindness that brought us to repentance. It was Jesus' compassion that brought about miracles. Put them on today and see the difference they make!

Colossians 3:12
"...clothe yourselves with compassion, kindness,
humility, gentleness and patience."

Your e... ...rll see...
In His beauty and...
...that stretches...
...behar...
...d satisfy the...
...then your lig...Clothe yourselves...
...and your...ndness, humilit...
...noon d...rince.

**most of what
you learn,
you learn via
offence**

$\mathcal{So}$ much is learnt in life by responding the right way to offence. Spiritual authority is gained by choosing the right response. The right response is to decide to sacrifice your own reputation and to trust God over the affairs of your future. We just need to commit ourselves again to the purposes of God and continue to do good.

Psalm 4:5
"Offer right sacrifices and trust in the Lord."

promotion
comes from
staying
hidden

Promotion is something we need to firmly take off our agenda and place back into God's hands. Promotion and exaltation come from God and not from personality or prominence, or being in the right places at the right time. The promotion of your life is surely on God's agenda, but in His time and in His way. He is never late, wrong, sexist or prejudiced in His plans. The key is to stay hidden until He is ready.

Psalm 138:8
"...the Lord will fulfil His purpose for me."

you are not working for crowns in this life - you are to be **rewarded** with crowns in the next!

The beauty of all that we do for Him is that we are not working for earthly rewards that will rot and decay. Instead, for those who are willing to go the distance, He promises rewards in Heaven that will resound for all eternity. This life and all that it entails is just a mere heartbeat compared to the eternal rewards that await His faithful servants. With this we encourage ourselves that our reward is with Him.

1 Peter 5:4
"...and when the chief shepherd appears you will receive the crown of glory that will never fade away."

when you choose God as your **protection** it is His responsibility to protect you

When you have deliberately chosen to be in someone's protection it is totally their responsibility to protect you. God is your protector. He is vigilant in carrying out His job. He justifies you, upholds your cause and fights your corner. He is the best of the best of security guards. He totally surrounds and enfolds you.

Ruth 2:12
"May you be richly rewarded by the Lord, the God of Israel, under whose wings you have come to take refuge."

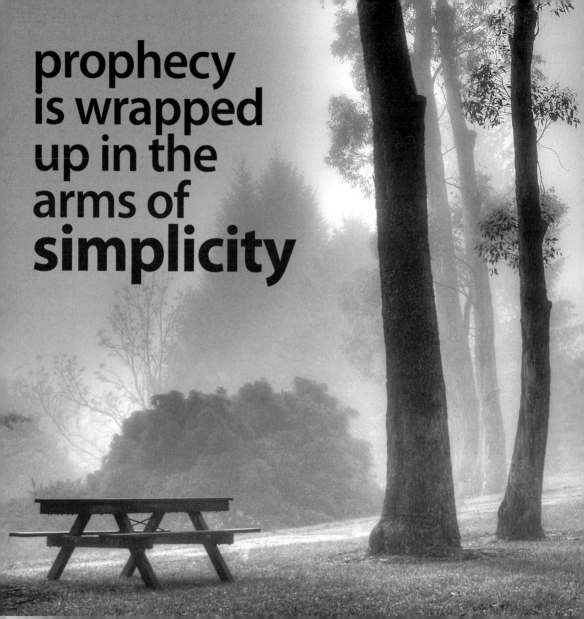

prophecy
is wrapped
up in the
arms of
simplicity

My God is not a God who is shrouded in mystery and complexity. He is a God who is natural and approachable, simple yet profound. His words are clear and uncluttered and within the grasp of common man. His ways are not so high that they are unintelligible and incoherent. He speaks simply, profoundly and correctly. The simple truth of His ways stuns the 'wise' into submission and brings the 'strongman' to naught.

1 Corinthians 1:27
"God chose the foolish things of the world to shame the wise. God chose the weak things of the world to shame the strong."

I plant the seed
of my little life
- He raises it
powerfully

When we plant the seed of our lives we plant seed that, at best, is impoverished, weak and tainted. The amazing thing, however, is that once planted in the hands of God, it does not develop earthiness, weakness and carnality. God instead gives life to the seed of our lives as He determines. He makes our impoverished seed glorious, powerful and spiritual. For once when we plant a seed - we don't get what we sow.

1 Corinthians 15:42-44
"The body that is sown is perishable; it is raised imperishable, it is sown in dishonour; it is raised in glory; it is sown in weakness, it is raised in power; it is sown a natural body, it is raised a spiritual body."

weakness is God's
opportunity to display
His strength

Our weakness is God's perfect opportunity to display not only His power but His heart towards us. He promises that He will not only deliver us once, but that He will come back to deliver us from ourselves time and time again. He just keeps faithfully coming back for more. He keeps delivering us, and keeps delivering us and keeps delivering us ... until that day when we are finally delivered into His presence.

2 Corinthians 4:14
"... because we know that the one who raised the Lord Jesus from the dead will also raise us with Jesus and present us with you in His presence."

Excellence in the house of God and the intelligence of studious strategists are mere tools for the power of the Holy Spirit. No Godly goal can be attained by any tool purely created by man alone. Natural effort is the poor relation to the supernatural power of the Holy Ghost to bring about change.

Galatians 3:3
"Are you so foolish? After beginning with the Spirit, are you now trying to attain your goal by human effort?"

don't get
picked
before
you're ripe

A blessed son or daughter of God spends their time by the streams of living water, constantly gaining sustenance. Then in the right season and at the right time, they yield their fruit. If you bear fruit in the wrong season, the fruit will not be good. It will be tasteless, spoilt or mutated. Don't get picked before you are ripe, stay connected to the tree, planted by the streams of living water.

Psalm 1:3
"He is like a tree planted by streams of living water, which yields its fruit in season, and whose leaf does not wither. Whatever he does prospers."

God wants to capture your
imagination

God wants to capture our imaginings. May our imagination be full of the God possibilities for our lives and those around us. May we be filled with God's imagination for our own lives, God's imagination for our church, God's imagination for our city and Gods imagination for our family. We know that when God gets a hold of our dreams, it will show us the true extent of His dream for humanity.

Jeremiah 33:3
"Call unto me and I will answer you, and I will tell you great and unsearchable things you do not know."

a train of **thought** is a train that takes you from one place to the next

When we catch a train we need to check where it's heading - it's exact destination. We need to be aware of our thought processes that have the power to take us both to good and bad destinations. There is always a fare to pay - a price for either journey. Better to be careful and choose the train (of thought) that uplifts, edifies and sends you on your way to a faith-filled, joy-enhanced destination. There's two trains leaving right now - one to 'Grimville', the other to 'Gladville'. All aboard the right train!

Romans 12:2
"But be transformed by the renewing of your mind."

there is no gauge on which you
can **measure** popularity

Everybody had something to say about Jesus. He was liked one day and disliked the next. He was hailed as a prophet then denied for healing on a holy day. Some people wanted to make Him king by force and others wanted to stone Him. He knew that no barometer or gauge of popularity told Him who He was. He knew who and whose He was. Have confidence in who God has said that you are. Have a heart of confidence.

John 6:15
"Jesus, knowing that they intended to come and make Him king by force, withdrew again to a mountain by Himself."

see **crisis**
as your best friend

When it seems like you have been stripped back to bare bones, take heart. God loves to use crisis as a means of developing new fruit in your life. Crisis is God's opportunity for you. From the very bones of your life will come new ministry, new opportunity and a total reliance on God Himself. The purity of God flows easily out of a broken vessel. New life and new fruit come out of a well pruned tree.

Isaiah 11:1
"A shoot will come up from the stump of Jesse, from his roots a branch will bear fruit."

don't fight the
season - reap
its harvest

Embrace each season of your life with zest. There is a special harvest awaiting you in every season of life. Don't shadow box and try to find a way out of where you are right now. Instead, trust that God is doing something awesome in and around you. When you have embraced the season, both the voice of God and the will of God for the way ahead will become unmistakable.

Isaiah 30:20-21
"Although the Lord gives you the bread of adversity and the water of affliction, your teachers will be hidden no more.... Whether you turn to the right or to the left, your ears will hear a voice behind you saying, 'This is the way, walk in it'."

embrace
the
future
with both
hands

There is a future out there for all of us that God wants us to embrace in our hearts. From the place of faith over our future we see a pleasant, prosperous and fruitful land. From the place of fear and dread we imagine a future full of obstacles and lack. God wants us to look directly into His face and to see that His plans for us are not just good; they are amazing. We then need to embrace our future with our heart, mouth and action. Bring it on!

Isaiah 33:17
"Your eyes will see the King in His beauty and view a land that stretches afar."

the **timing** of God is the line between striving and the will of God

For us, any time is right. Any time seems a good time. Many times we try to push through doors and completely miss what God is saying. Jesus had to wait many times because the timing was not yet in place. Better to wait and hit the mark than to launch and frustrate yourself through lack of fruit.

John 7:6
"The right time for Me has not yet come.
For you any time is right."

God's love is **softly** written on the paper of your heart

There is something so tender about the way God writes His love upon the paper of our hearts. He gently etches who He is through His word and the touch of His presence. He hears and He answers our heartfelt prayers and responds with understanding to the deep longings of our heart. He bottles up our tears and draws us on lovingly into a deeper friendship with the living God. How our souls are loved.

1 John 4:16
"And so we know and rely on the love God has for us. God is love."

never
underestimate
the **power**
of prayer

The greatest thing anyone can do for man and God is to pray. Our enemy hates it when we pray. He knows it is our divine connection with the supernatural. Prayer is not so much about feeling good but about seeing other's lives touched and changed. We need to pray with perseverance until we see the breakthrough. Real prayer is vital to our cause. The defining line between success and failure is prayer.

James 5:16
"...The prayer of a righteous man is powerful and effective."

thankfulness
is a powerful tool

So much stems out of thankfulness. We need to be people who make a practice of thanking God even when we don't feel like it. This honours Him. This decision to honour God through a thankful heart prepares the highway for the salvation of God. Thankfulness prepares the four lane highway upon which God can fast track all the provision of Heaven.

Psalm 50:23
"He who sacrifices thank offerings, honours me..."

you are no
called to jostl
for position
- you ar
called to pass
something
amazing
on

We are not called to establish a mark for ourselves in this life but instead to pass on an amazing inheritance. We need to be genuinely thrilled when those behind us get hold of the faith life and excel in its execution. The continuity of all you have learned lies in making other people great.

Proverbs 13:22
"A good man leaves an inheritance for his children's children."

God has a specific purpose for each individual life. We were never intended to try to mimic someone else's destiny. We will make, at best, a bad copy of another's purpose and, at worst, a complete disaster. God's rewards in Heaven are for those who grab hold of what God has for them and who run with it wholeheartedly, no matter how 'small' that destiny may appear.

Psalm 57:2
"...to God, who fulfils His purpose for me."

God wants to
hear the
inner voice
of your heart

God really wants to hear about the inner you. He wants to hear you express to Him the joys, concerns and secrets of your heart. He wants to hear the heartbeat of the real you that separates you from every other person He has created. There is nothing that delights a Father's heart more than a child who is truly herself in His company.

Psalm 27:8
"My heart says of you, 'Seek His face'. Your face Lord I will seek."

some
things
God
forgets
- other
things
He
doesn't

God removes your sins and your failings and washes them away in the sea of forgetfulness. However, He doesn't forget your labour, your love and your prayers. He stands in Heaven cheering you on and He is always thankful that you have chosen to continue to serve and love Him. He doesn't forget when, against all the odds and when exhausted, persecuted and frustrated, you continue to love His people.

Hebrews 6:10
"God is not unjust. He will not forget your work and the love you have shown Him as you have helped His people and continue to help them."

God will not be
tender towards
you in an area that
will ruin your life

There are some quagmires we get ourselves into that God yanks us out of. He doesn't tenderly speak to us to step out of it because He knows it is not a good place for us. When we realise God is committed to building us and not devastating us, His discipline becomes a delight not a chore. Just like a parent, God has both a tender touch and a strong hand. Be aware, He will use both on your life.

Hebrews 12:5-6
"Do not make light of the Lord's discipline and do not lose heart when He rebukes you, because the Lord disciplines those He loves."

lean up against the big wall of **faith**

When you have fought the good fight of faith and have run a great race, there is a time when you just need to go and lean. Time to lean against the big wall of faith and to rest in the arms of the One who is bigger than you. He is the One who holds it all in all. You gain your strength and reinvigoration from settling down in complete dependence on a big God.

Isaiah 30:15
"In repentance and rest is your salvation. In quietness and trust is your strength."

knowing
your
personal
value brings
confidence

When you know your own personal value to God, it develops a confidence in you that Heaven wants you to walk in. Having confidence means you give a sense of value away to others. It gives you the power to give something awesome away. God-confidence gives you strength in relationships and the power to succeed in your God-given pursuits. Knowing your value reflects well on others.

Proverbs 31: 11
"Her husband has full confidence in her and lacks nothing of value"

At times it would be easy to believe that your life is determined by the boundaries of your personal ability. The boundaries God has set for you (and for the lives of all you love) stretch way beyond the barriers of ability, history and education. They stretch out into the expansive territory fenced only by the amazing plans He has for us. When we place ourselves in the hands of God, neither talent nor the opinions of men determine destiny. It is God who outworks the plan for our lives.

Proverbs 16: 9
"In his heart a man plans his course, but the Lord determines his steps."

you can't **fight** your corner of the Kingdom in someone else's armour

It is easy to try and copy those around us in our quest for greatness and spiritual things. We are, however, not only uncomfortable in someone else's gear, but totally useless for fulfilling our own unique calling. The best weapon that God has in his armoury is you - you fighting the battle with the sling and five smooth stones that you are accustomed to. You are then no longer cumbersome in battle, but agile and accurate.

1 Samuel 17: 39
"I cannot go in these' he said to Saul, 'because I am not used to them.' So he took them off."

Out of the rubble of our lives God creates amazing beauty. He fashions such beauty out of total devastation. He takes our pain, our sorrow and the scar no man can heal and, with a brushstroke of His love, He brushes over them forever. In their place He creates an artwork in our lives that is a true reflection of all the glories of Heaven. Our brokenness becomes the canvas for His masterpiece.

Isaiah 61: 3
"...to bestow on them a crown of beauty instead of ashes."

it was your **exceptiona**
affliction that allowed God
to make you into the person
you've become

When people admire your status, your influence, your armour and your life, remember that it is only the grace of God that has allowed you to be who you are today. When you have been so mightily delivered you cannot for a moment attribute who you are today to your own power or decision making. God is amazing in the way He uses what was once despised and lowly to reflect the greatness of the God of the universe.

1 Corinthians 1: 26-28
"...think of what you were when you were called. Not many were of noble birth. But God chose the foolish things of the world to shame the wise. God chose the weak things... He chose the lowly things... and the despised things."

**your services
are required
by Me**

Your unique services are required by the King. He calls us before His throne and wants us to dissolve our excuses and remove our 'get out' clauses. He wants us to put aside our insecurities and self-doubt and realise we are particularly made for His service. Only you can serve God in the way He needs you to. Your life is needed in particular. This day, your life is needed in immediate responsiveness to the directive of the King.

Galatians 1: 15
"But when God, who set me apart from birth, and called me by His grace..."

your star is
still rising
because I am
defending
you

Your life is the most frustrating thing to those who oppose you. Somehow or other your life just keeps rising from the ashes - even the ashes of unjustified attack. Your star is still rising because your defender is strong. Your hope will not be cut off because God, powerful and mighty, is committed to fighting your corner. You are kept safe and hidden by His strength.

Proverbs 23: 10-11
"... or encroach on the fields of the fatherless, for their defender is strong. He will take up their case against you."

trust happens
when you can't
see what lies
ahead

To know that you trust God is to know deep in your heart that God Himself is in your present and your future - when you can't see what's actually ahead. Trusting God happens when you can't understand what is happening right now but you don't succumb to panic. Trust happens when you can't even feel the Master's touch but you know that He who is invisible is still with you. That is trust.

Isaiah 50: 10
"...trust in the name of the Lord and rely on his God"

all God
wants is a
pliable
heart

God does not delight in you being a superstar. He does not delight in you displaying incredible strength, amazing talent or jaw-dropping authority. What God loves to see within us is a pliable heart. A heart that is open to direction. A soft heart. He loves a heart that is easily moved and is willing to fulfil the agenda of the King of Heaven.

Psalm 51: 17
"The sacrifices of God are a broken spirit, a broken and contrite heart."

you have to find a **home** before you invite others in

You need to find your place of comfort close to the heart of God. That is the place where you will experience His love, His touch and His power. They are all waiting for you there. Once this place becomes a home for you and not a hotel, you can give out strength and authority, joy and peace from that strong settlement that you have made in your heart. Make your home today in the heart of Heaven.

Psalm 84: 3
"Even the sparrow has found a home, and the swallow a nest for herself. Where she may have her young - a place near Your altar."

it's time to
champion
the cause of the
unlovely

It is our mandate as God's people on the planet to go out of our way for the unloved and the dispossessed. God promises that when we provide for those who are incapable or paralysed to provide for themselves, then His light and salvation will shine for you - brighter and brighter. It is time to fight for those who cannot fight for themselves, to not just visit their cause but to champion it.

Isaiah 58: 10
"If you spend yourselves on behalf of the hungry, and satisfy the needs of the oppressed, then your light will rise in the darkness and your night will become the noonday."

watch out for the
still **small voice**
of the unexplained

If I'd been organising the event of Jesus riding into Jerusalem, a donkey's colt would not have been my chosen mode of transport. Yet the Redeemer of mankind rode in on the back of an unassuming animal. Your King often comes to you in the most unusual, unexpected and unassuming ways. Be aware that all the power of Heaven comes to you housed in the unexpected.

John 12:15
"Do not be afraid, O daughter of Zion. See your King is coming seated on a donkey's colt."

peace is not the absence of adversity **peace** is knowing God in adversity

Trouble does not mean you are out of the will of God. Real peace is finding footsteps in the midst of adversity. Peace is not finding a retreat away from the thud of battle. Real peace is staying firmly put on the battlefront with an unnatural sense of God firmly upon you. Peace is knowing God's hand will never leave you and will lead you out into an even more spacious place.

John 14:27
"Peace I leave with you; my peace I give you. I do not give to you as the world gives. Do not let your hearts be troubled and do not be afraid."

cast at the
right place

If you throw the net of your life in the right direction you will have an awesome catch. In the right direction we attract amazing God favour. God promises that even when we have a huge catch, the fragile net of your life will not even be torn. Your strength and capacity will increase to house the catch. He will equip you with both strength and an ability to know the right place to fish.

John 21:6
"'Throw your net on the right side of the boat and you will find some.' When they did they were unable to haul the net in because of the large number of fish."

also available in
the **DEVOTIONAL RESCUE** series